Flavors of
Italy

Flavors of
Italy

Clare Ferguson

photography by **Jeremy Hopley**

COURAGE
BOOKS

AN IMPRINT OF RUNNING PRESS
PHILADELPHIA • LONDON

Designer **Megan Smith**

Design Assistant **Stuart Edwards**

Editor **Elsa Petersen-Schepelern**

Creative Director **Jacqui Small**

Publishing Director **Anne Ryland**

Production **Meryl Silbert**

Food Stylist **Clare Ferguson**

Stylist **Wei Tang**

Photographer's Assistant **Catherine Rowlands**

Indexer **Hilary Bird**

Author Photograph **Graeme Harris**

Dedication
To my husband, Ian Ferguson, for his encouragement.

Acknowledgements
My thanks to Jeremy Hopley, Wei Tang, Catherine Rowlands, Nicky Rogerson, Karl Rixon, Megan Smith, Elsa Petersen-Schepelern, and Fiona Smith—The A Team. Thanks to David Turcchi and Christine Boodle for technical advice, Lina Stores, Soho (especially Franco and Toni), Giovanni and Sara of Speck, Holland Park, Salvatore Maggiulli and Marcello Bizia at Salumeria Napoli, Battersea, and Julia Montenelli for her help with the translations. Thanks also to my suppliers; butchers David Lidgate and Kingsland, and greengrocers the Michanicou Brothers and Hyams & Cockerton. Particular thanks are due to Angelo Conte of Fine Italian Foods, London, for his help in supplying the high-quality dried pasta produced by De Cecco. My appreciation also to my agents Fiona Lindsay and Linda Shanks.

Notes
**All spoon measurements are level unless otherwise specified.
Ovens should be preheated to the specified temperature. If using
a convection oven, adjust times and temperature according to the
manufacturer's instructions.**

© Ryland Peters & Small, 1998
First published in the United States of America in 1998 by Courage Books

10 9 8 7 6 5 4 3 2 1
Digit on the right indicates the number of this printing

Library of Congress Cataloging-in-Publication number 97-77956

ISBN 0-7624-0360-8
This book may be ordered by mail from the publisher
But try your bookshop first!

Published by Courage Books, an imprint of
Running Press Book Publishers
125 South Twenty-second Street
Philadelphia, Pennsylvania 19103-4399

contents

introduction

From the northern Alps to the southernmost tip of Sicily, Italy provides tangible proof that the world is a stage: the Italians (only united since 1871 as a nation), have a sparkle, vivacity, an amused elegance, lust for life, and style that is almost theatrical. It ranges from the non-stop hustle and bustle of street life to the slower pace of the country.

For Italians, the conviviality of the table has always been the cornerstone of family life. Italians believe that eating, drinking, and living are enhanced by celebrating the innate deliciousness of each ingredient, and their cooking has much less blending, merging, and modifying of flavors than many of the other great cuisines. The food sings with freshness, vividness, brilliance of pure color and flavor.

Allegria—the happiness felt when sharing good things with friends, family, or colleagues—runs through life and cooking.

Time-honored techniques are protected and encouraged, but melded with state-of-the-art tools, technology, and agriculture. Many classic Italian dishes adapt easily to today's lighter, quicker, simpler, healthier eating patterns. The so-called "Mediterranean Diet" is simply a way of life for Italians—an ongoing passion for good olive oil, bread, wine, olives, dried beans, grains, and fresh vegetables.

Today even ordinary families still sit down to a first course (*primi piatti*), a second course (*secondi piatti*), and vegetables (*contorni*). Always there is wine, spring water, good local bread, and often cheese and fresh fruits. Many times (but not always) there will be a dessert (*dolce*), especially for feast days, holiday celebrations, name days, anniversaries, or to mark a special occasion. To finish, an espresso (*il caffè*) and perhaps a digestif (*liquore*) might bring the meal to its end.

My collection of recipes, together with a summary of vital techniques and essential ingredients, is but a taste of the joys Italy's gastronomy has to offer: go and explore *la cucina d'Italia* for yourself.

Italian ingredients

Much of the magic of Italian food is due to the quality of its ingredients, which are produced, chosen, and used with intense interest, passion, and pride. Though regional produce varies hugely and methods of cooking are diverse, there are some ingredients which are integral to all Italian cooking styles. The following examples are a few of the essentials.

1

4

6

ITALIAN HERBS

1. Herbs are signature flavoring ingredients in Italian cooking. Back row, from left:
Italian flat-leaf parsley is used cooked or fresh. Thought superior to curly parsley.
Marjoram has a sweeter scent than **oregano** (the wild version). Dried oregano can be used in winter instead of fresh marjoram.
Basil is best when grown in hot sun. Large-leaved sweet basil is the most common, and its intense, spicy scent characterizes many dishes. Purple or opal basil is also grown.
Front row, from left: Tarragon has intense, aniseed flavor, used in salsa verde and with some boiled meats in Florence and Siena.
Sage has a musky, pungent scent, good with pork, poultry, liver, broils, beans, and, when deep-fried in oil, as a garnish.
Bay leaf has a lemon-nutmeg flavor. It is removed before serving or eating.
Rosemary has intensely aromatic evergreen leaves, used with broiled, roasted, and barbecued food, as well as in stuffings.

VEGETABLES AND SALADS

2. Artichokes, clockwise from left, include:
Globe artichoke is the flower of a thistle-like plant. Eaten whole when very young, served raw in salad, with vinaigrette, or cooked with accompaniments. When older or larger, the interior "choke" is large and prickly, so only the leaf bases and heart are eaten.
Jerusalem artichoke (right) is a crisp tuber, served thinly sliced when raw. Boiled or baked, it is served as a soup or with sauce.

3. Florence fennel is an aniseed-flavored vegetable, served raw in salads or lightly cooked as an appetizer or accompaniment for fish, poultry, or meats.

4. Cabbages, clockwise from left:
Cavolo nero or black cabbage has a strong, earthy flavor. Fashionable and still rare, though becoming more widely available—Savoy cabbage may be substituted.
Cime de rapa or turnip greens have a bitter, nutty taste, chewy texture. Beet leaves, wild chicory, dandelion, arugula, spinach beet, or Swiss chard may be used instead.
Blanched chicory blanched by growing it in the dark. Prized for its clean, bitter flavor. Used like spinach, or for stuffing pastas such as tortelloni.

5. An infinite variety of mushrooms is used in Italy, with wild mushrooms being particularly prized. Markets have highly trained officials who identify safe wild mushrooms before sale. From left:
Porcini fresh (left) and dried (right) are in season from high summer to autumn. Known as *ceps* in France, they have an intense, almost meaty taste and are highly prized. Dried porcini should be reconstituted for about 30 minutes in boiling water before use. The soaking water is also used. Other wild mushrooms are widely available in Italy, as are farmed mushrooms.
Chanterelles (rear), known as *galetti* in Italy, have a nutty flavor and chewy texture.

6. **Italian tomatoes** are intensely flavorful and include, clockwise from top left:

Salad tomatoes are large, often irregularly shaped, red and green blotched. Very flavorful. (So-called "beefsteak" tomatoes, though similar in appearance, often lack the flavor prized by Italians.)

Cherry tomatoes are sweet-sharp, used raw in uncooked salsas and in cooked sauces, on pizzas, and with toasted breads.

Plum or Roma tomatoes are not very juicy, but intensely fleshy. Good for cooking. Often peeled or roasted, then added to composite dishes or pulped to form passato.

Sun-dried tomatoes with their intense, meaty taste, are sold dry (to be rehydrated in hot water or stock) or packed in good olive oil with herbs and seasonings. Sun-dried tomato paste is a useful condiment.

7. **Italian salad leaves** are numerous and varied. Wild leaves (*insalata di campo*) are gathered by householders from fields and roadside verges. Cultivated varieties widely available outside Italy include, clockwise from top left:

Radicchio or red chicory has a nutty, slightly bitter taste. Used raw, in salads, or as an accompaniment, broiled or braised.

Trevise is a long-leafed version of radicchio, used in salads, stews, or with roasts.

Rucola is known as rocket in Britain, Australia and New Zealand, *roquette* in France and *arugula* in Spain and America. Eaten raw when young, or cooked as a vegetable when older.

8. **Garlic** is used both fresh and young, fresh and mature, or dried and mature.

Young garlic is mild and sticky, older garlic has a strong, intense flavor, especially when dried. Used raw or cooked. Cloves in older bulbs often have an interior green shoot, which is strong and bitter in taste. The shoot should be removed before use.

1

2

3

ITALIAN CHEESES

1. Soft cheeses, used in cooking or eaten fresh, include, from left:

Ricotta (not strictly a cheese) is white, mild, crumbly, high in moisture, adaptable, used in gnocchi, stuffings, cakes, and desserts.

Mascarpone (front) is fresh, thick, white cow's milk cheese with creamy texture. Eaten straight in sweet or savory dishes, salted in sauces, dressings, stuffings, or with polenta, and as a dessert stirred with sugar, liqueur, and other flavorings.

Mozzarella is a soft, mild cheese, low in fat, sold in its own whey. Melts well and binds ingredients. Often used raw in salads. In Campania, the version made from rich buffalo milk (*mozzarella di bufala*) is considered finer than the cow's milk version.

2. Italian hard cheeses include, from top:

Pecorino Romano (top) sheep's milk cheese from central and southern Italy. Strong, peppery flavor. Grate, cook or eat as it is.

Other pecorino cheeses, (second row, from left) **Peperino, Sardo,** and **Sardo extra mature**. When fresh, they are known as *fresco*, when aged, as *stagionato*. Strong, peppery and pungent. Grate, cook, or eat as it is.

Parmigiano-Reggiano (front left) is widely available and used fresh, grated, cooked, and as a condiment. *Nuovo* is young and soft, *vecchio* matured and *stravecchio* oldest, matured for 3 years.

Grana Padano (front right) is a similar cheese, used raw or as cooking condiment.

3. Other cooking cheeses include, from rear:

Provoloncino (rear) White or straw-coloured medium hard *pasta filata* cheese. Available as mild (*dolce*), sharp (*piccante*), and smoked (*affumicato*). Nutty, sweet, mild, good for eating fresh, as well as cooking.

Provolone (front left) is made by the *pasta filata (stretched curd)* method, formerly from buffalo milk, sometimes now from cow's milk. Usually made in bulbous shapes, it is now also available in disks, from which this wedge has been cut. The *dolce* version here is mild, smooth, aged for only 2 months.

Fontina (center) is a medium-soft cow's milk cheese, pale gold, nutty, subtle, melts creamily, so good in fondues and sauces.

Gorgonzola (right) is a blue-veined cheese, good for eating as is, and for melting and cooking. Dolcelatte (not shown) is a milder and younger version.

4. Italian sausages for cooking from top:
Zampone is a pig's trotter stuffed with pork sausage meat. Sold uncooked in Italy, pre- or part-cooked outside Italy. **Luganega** of raw, coarse-ground pork, spices, herbs, and sometimes cheese. Pan-grilled, barbecued, or broken and used in pasta sauces. **Cotechino** sold uncooked in Italy, pre- or part-cooked outside Italy, shrink-wrapped in boxes. Like zampone, it is usually poached and served with lentils or polenta.

5. Salame are cured sausages, made all over Italy, the spicier and hotter the further south you go. Of the hundreds of varieties made, shown here, clockwise from top left, are: **Mortadella** is a fine, mild pork sausage with lard, garlic, peppercorns, and sometimes pistachios. It is used in antipasti or salads. Shown whole are the strong and peppery **Abruzzese** and the mild and sweet **Milano**. Shown sliced are **Zia Ferrarese** (with strong garlic taste), **Stofolotto** (mild tasting and coarsely textured), and **Finocchiona,** flavored with fennel seeds. The strings of mini salame are **Bocconcini del Cacciatore**—*bocconcini* means "little mouthfuls." Salame are best sliced to order by the shopkeeper, to be eaten immediately—do not store. However, if bought whole, they can be stored for months if kept in a cool dry place.

6. Italian cured meats are served alone, as part of antipasti, or in recipes as a flavoring, clockwise from bottom left: **Pancetta coppata** and **affumicata** are unsmoked and smoked Italian bacon. **Prosciutto crudo di Parma** is raw, salted, cured ham. **Prosciutto Cotto** is cooked ham. **Bresaola** is unsmoked, cured beef or venison cut into thin slices. **Coppa** is pork shoulder, rolled and cured with salt, pepper, nutmeg. **Prosciutto crudo di San Daniele** like Parma, is raw, salted, and cured.

5

6

1

2

3

4

5

SPICES AND CONDIMENTS

1. The truffle, an underground fungus, is one of the world's most prized and expensive ingredients. Its scent is absorbed by other foods such as rice, polenta, eggs, and pasta. Black truffles are found in Umbria, the white in Piedmont. Clockwise from right:
Fresh truffles are in season in autumn.
Preserved truffle and **truffle oil** are available throughout the year. Use sparingly.

2. Liqueurs and spirit used in cooking, from left:
Marsala is a fragrant fortified Sicilian wine, used as Madeira is in French cooking. Use

Marsala Superiore—never *all'uovo* (egg).
Grappa is a clear grape spirit, fiery, slightly smoky at times. Substitute marc or slivovitz. Others (not shown) include Noci (from walnuts) and Amaretto (from almonds).

3. Perhaps the most important flavoring ingredients in Italian cooking, from left:
Olive oil use lesser-quality oils, such as virgin, for cooking. Use cold-pressed (extra-virgin) olive oil for salads and dressings. Estate-bottled first pressings are often exorbitantly priced, but even supermarkets now sell respectable extra-virgin olive oil.

Balsamic vinegar is a special aged vinegar, used sparingly as a seasoning or flavoring Wine vinegar is used for most purposes.
Olives for eating and cooking are picked unripe (green) or tree-ripened (purplish-brown to dark). Cured in salt, brine, or oil.

4. Salt and acid flavors include, from right:
Capers are the buds of a Mediterranean wall plant, best when tiny. Eaten raw, sun-dried, and salted (right) or pickled (left). Rinse, pat dry, and use immediately.
Anchovies are small salted fish, sold loose, or in bottles or cans, and in either salt

6

(second from left) or olive oil (rear left). All taste intense, sweet, and salty, used as a condiment, with pizza, stuffings, and sauces.

5. Nuts are widely used. Since their oils quickly turn rancid, they should be kept in the refrigerator. Shown from left:
Chestnuts are sold fresh in autumn, vacuum packed or dried throughout the year. Peeled by blanching, then while still hot removing the shell and inner membrane. Chestnut flour is used in baking.
Pignolis are the seeds from stone pine cones, hand-processed, so expensive. Used in pesto, sweet dishes, and baking.
Walnuts are used in sweet and savory dishes, and to make the liqueur, Noci. Now most walnuts come from the south, since those in the north were felled to replace furniture destroyed in World War II .
Almonds (not shown), sweet and bitter, are also important in Italy, being used in cookies (amaretti) and liqueur (Amaretto).

6. Spices common in Italian cooking include, clockwise from left:
Saffron strands are the dried golden-red stigmas of the saffron crocus grown in the Arbruzzo. Expensive and prized for its warm color and superb flavor. Strands are the best, but it is also available as **Saffron powder** (not shown)—Italian saffron powder is more reliable than other kinds.
Black pepper is always used freshly ground.
Chiles, fresh or (more commonly) dried are used to give flavor and spice, mostly in dishes from Southern Italy.
Nutmeg (front) and **Mace** (right) are favorite, pungent spices used often in sauces and with spinach. Mace is the dried lacy covering of the nutmeg. Its flavor is similar to nutmeg, but subtler and milder.

DRIED PASTA

Dried pasta is made by mixing water and hard-wheat durum flour into a paste (pasta), shaped in hundreds of ways, then dried. It was particularly identified with Southern Italy but is now universal. It is boiled until *al dente* (firm to the tooth) and served with oil-based sauces, tomato sauces, or other dressings. The romantic names of pasta shapes describe their origins or shapes.

1. Pasta lunga (long pasta), from left:
Bucatoni (big holes), **Linguine** (little tongues), and **Spaghetti** (strings).

2. Fettuce (ribbons) include, from left:
Tagliolini (little cuts), **Tagliatelle** (thin cuts), **Fettucine** (little ribbons), and **Pappardelle** (wide noodles).

3. Tubi (tube-shaped), clockwise from top left:
Cannelloni, usually boiled, stuffed with sauces, then baked, **Rigatoni, Penne** (pens or quills), **Maccheroni Rigati,** and **Chifferi Rigati** or elbow macaroni. *Rigato* means ridged: the ridges help hold the sauces.

4. Forme Speciali (special shapes) include, clockwise from left:
Hand-made **Strozzapreti** (priest-stranglers), **Lumache Rigate Grandi** (big snails with ridged surface), **Farfalle** (butterflies/bowties), **Conchiglie Rigate** (shells with ridged surface), and **Orecchiette** (little ears).

5. Forme Speciali (special shapes) include corkscrews and wheels, from left:
Fusilli (twists), **Rotelle** (little wheels), and **Eliche** (spirals).

6. Lasagne and Soup Pastas include:
Sheets of **spinach lasagne** noodles on top of **plain lasagne** noodles. Also the soup pastas **stellette** (little stars) and **orzi** (barley grains).

7. Pasta Colorata (colored pasta):
In Italy only (from top) squid ink, spinach, and tomato pastas are considered acceptable. Outside Italy, beet, basil, mushroom, and other flavored pastas are also available.

ITALIAN RICE AND FLOUR
Italian cooks use the grains and flours commonly used in the West, but also use versions specific to Italy.

8. Grain products include, from left:
Risotto rice Italy produces over 50 types of this round-grained starchy grain that cooks to a sticky, creamy consistency. *Ordinario* is the most common, while the best-quality are Carnaroli, Vialone nano, and Arborio.

Italian flour is made from durum (hard grain or *grano duro*) wheat, used for pasta flour. There are 5 categories, ranging from white and silky typo 00 to *integrale*—whole wheat flour. Typo 00 has been used in this book to make fresh pasta, but all-purpose is used in other recipes, unless otherwise specified.

Polenta is yellow cornmeal. Sometimes used to make bread, but is usually boiled and served as wet polenta or dried and broiled, char-grilled, baked, or deep-fried.

PULSES AND LEGUMES
9. Beans, peas, and lentils include, from left:
Ceci (chickpeas), sold dried, are pale yellow to buff in color. Check date limit—avoid stale chickpeas. Also sold in cans and jars, ready to eat. Mealy, nutty, and adaptable, used in soups, stews, and purées.

Castelluccio lentils are the Italian version of best-quality French *Lentilles de Puy*. Tiny, grey-green quick-cook, no-soak lentils are served alone or as an accompaniment to fish, game, meat, and sausages such as zampone and cotechino.

Borlotti beans are cream in color, with red-brown spots. Sold fresh in fall, dried at other seasons, or canned. Usually served as accompaniment for meat, poultry, or game, or in soups and in stews. Sweet and mild.

Cannellini beans are pale in color, with a mild and nutty flavor. They must be soaked and cooked without salt—salt makes beans tough, and so should be added towards the end of cooking time. Flavored with herbs, olive oil, or garlic, and use in purées, soups, or cooked with sausage. Also sold canned.

Making pasta

Making egg-based pasta at home is not a complicated exercise. The dough can be made quickly using a food processor then rolled out using a hand-cranked pasta machine (the one most people use). Cook it in boiling salted water for just a few minutes—when it's ready, the pasta will rise to the surface.

Ingredients

1½ cups Italian pasta flour (typo 00) or all-purpose flour

⅛ teaspoon salt

2 medium eggs

2 medium egg yolks

3 tablespoons semolina, for rolling

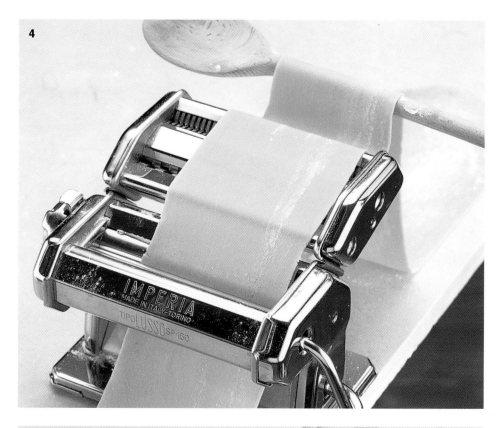

4

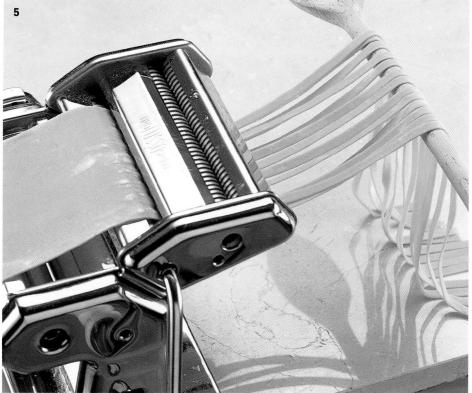

5

1. Making the dough

Put the first 4 ingredients in a food processor. Process in short bursts until the dough comes together to form a ball.

2. Kneading and resting

Transfer the dough onto a surface dusted with semolina. Knead it until smooth and silky—about 3 to 4 minutes. Divide the dough into two and wrap both balls in plastic. Chill for 30 minutes or up to 2 hours.

3. Rolling the dough

To roll out the pasta dough, pat one ball into a long, flat disk shape. Following the pasta machine instructions, feed the dough through the rollers (set wide) folding the rolled dough into 3, giving it a right-angled turn and repeating the process at least 4 to 8 more times.

4. Thinning the pasta

Roll the pasta through the machine several times and gradually narrow the gap between the rollers until the thinnest is reached. Loop the dough carefully, as it emerges from the rollers. Stop when the pasta is thin, silky, and fine (for ravioli you should be able to read newsprint through it).

5. Cutting the pasta

If making cut pasta, fit the trenette wheel and feed the pasta through the machine. Drape the cut pasta over a pasta horse or doweling rods and let dry until leathery, or cover, refrigerated, for up to 24 hours.

6. Cooking the pasta (not shown)

See step 3, overleaf. Bring a large pan of salted water to the boil, add the pasta, return to a boil, and cook until the pasta rises to the surface (1 to 2 minutes). Drain, transfer to a pasta plate and add your choice of sauce. A few spoonfuls of cooking water are often added to the sauce.

Making filled pasta

Fresh filled pastas include round or square ravioli, half-moon shaped raviolini, triangular panzotti, and the square or ring-shaped tortelloni. Choose stuffings such as pumpkin (page 32) or ragù (page 21).

Ravioli
1 quantity fresh egg pasta (page 16)

1 lb. filling, divided into 16–20 portions

1 egg, beaten with 4 tablespoons water, to seal

6 tablespoons melted butter, or ½ cup other sauce, such as tomato, to serve

1. Adding the filling
Roll out 1 quantity fresh pasta (step 4, page 17) and spread flat on the work surface. Put 1 tablespoon of the filling at 2 to 3 inch intervals on the lower half. Brush the egg-water sealing glaze onto the dough around the fillings.

2. Sealing the ravioli
Fold the top section of dough over the top and press carefully to make a good seal and exclude air bubbles. Cut into squares with a fluted pasta cutter, or into circles with a 2-inch cutter. Discard the trimmings.

3. Cooking the pasta
Poach the ravioli a large saucepan of boiling stock or salted water until they rise to the surface. Continue cooking for about 2 to 4 minutes longer to ensure the filling is heated through, then remove from the water using a strainer or slotted spoon. Serve with a sauce of your choice.

1

Making polenta

Polenta, made from yellow cornmeal, is one of the great Italian accompaniments. It is served in two forms; wet, a little like mashed potatoes (page 54), or toasted, roasted, or char-grilled (page 42).

Wet Polenta
7 cups boiling beef or chicken stock
1⅓ cups coarse yellow cornmeal (polenta)
2 teaspoons salt, or to taste
2 tablespoons sweet butter

2

3

1. Cooking the polenta

Bring the stock to a boil in a large pan. Drizzle in the polenta in a steady stream, stirring in the same direction with a large metal whisk over a high heat. (It spatters, so wrap your arm and hand in a cloth!) Cook, stirring, for 25 to 30 minutes more to form a thick, lump-free "porridge." Add salt to taste, then the butter, and serve as wet polenta, or make dried polenta (Steps 2, 3).

2. Preparing dry polenta

Pour the wet polenta mixture onto a large wooden board to form a flat circle.

3. Cutting polenta

Let cool completely, then cut into wedges using a knife or taut thread.

4

4. Char-grilling or sautéeing polenta

Heat a skillet or stove-top grill pan until very hot. Brush the polenta wedges with olive oil, add to the pan, and press down onto the hot surface. Cook for 8 to 15 minutes until the crust is crisp. Turn over and cook the other side for 8 to 15 minutes more.

Italian sauces

condimenti italiani

Salsa di pomodoro Tomato Sauce

When the tomato arrived in Italy from the New World at the end of the 16th century, it was held in deep suspicion. The Neapolitans were among the first to try it. This is a quick everyday recipe which can be stored in the refrigerator with a film of oil on top, covered, until needed for use. The composition of this sauce changes from one area of Italy to another. In the south, for instance, dried chile flakes are used instead of the black pepper, reflecting its proximity to the great trade routes of the Mediterranean.

2 lb. very ripe, red tomatoes, such as plum or cherry tomatoes
12 fresh basil leaves, torn
a small handful of parsley, tied into a bunch
1 tablespoon black pepper (or 2 teaspoons chile flakes)
1 onion, chopped
4 garlic cloves, chopped
2 teaspoons salt
extra-virgin olive oil, to cover

Makes 4 cups

Chop the tomatoes. Put all the ingredients except the oil in a large heavy-bottom saucepan and bring to a boil. Simmer for about 30 minutes until very flavorful and reduced. Sieve carefully and pour into a clean heatproof jar or bowl. Drizzle over a film of olive oil. Cool then refrigerate. Use within 1 week.

Note: if preferred, purée the sauce in a blender and do not sieve.

Ragù Bolognese Meat Sauce

One of the greatest of all meat sauces. For a richer result, add ⅔ cup light cream and/or 8 oz. chicken livers.

8 oz. prosciutto crudo or cotto (cured or cooked ham)
1 onion, finely chopped
1 carrot, finely chopped
1 celery stalk, chopped
2 tablespoons unsalted butter, plus extra if using chicken livers
2 tablespoons virgin olive oil
3 cups finely ground meat such as beef, pork or a mixture
½ cup medium dry white wine
2 tablespoons tomato paste or sun-dried tomato paste
a small bunch of fresh bay leaves
1–1¼ cups boiling chicken or beef stock
½ teaspoon ground nutmeg
salt and freshly ground black pepper

Serves 6–8

Chop the prosciutto, onion, carrot, and celery together to form a fine, even mixture. Heat the butter in a large skillet, add the mixture, and sauté for about 6 to 8 minutes, stirring.

Heat the oil in a second skillet and brown the meat gently. Stir in the wine and cook until the liquid is almost evaporated. Add the tomato paste, the bay leaves, and stock. Add the onion mixture, stir, bring to a boil, cover, reduce the heat, and simmer for 35 to 45 minutes. (If including cream and/or chicken livers, add them now, mashing the livers well as they cook.)

Stir in nutmeg, salt, and pepper to taste, then serve.

Pesto Basil Sauce

Pesto, Italy's famous basil-scented sauce is related to other basil sauces of the Mediterranean, such as the *pistou* of Provence. Traditionally made with a mortar and pestle, it is now more often made in a food processor.

5 garlic cloves, crushed
½ cup pignoli nuts
4 large handfuls fresh basil (stems and leaves), torn or chopped
¼ cup grated Pecorino Sardo or Parmigiano-Reggiano (Parmesan)
⅔ cup virgin olive oil
2 tablespoons ricotta or fromage frais (optional)
sea salt

Serves 6–8

Pound the garlic and pignolis in a mortar and pestle with a few pinches of salt to help the grinding process. Pound in the basil, a quarter at a time. Pound in the cheese until well mixed. Beat in the olive oil to make a thick, creamy paste, then beat in the ricotta or fromage frais. Keep in a cool place—but do not refrigerate. Pesto can also be made in a food processor, using a metal blade and working in the same order. Do not over-process.

The gastronomy of Italy is a joy and a delight, not least because it has stayed so passionately regional over the centuries and yet has been able to absorb and integrate outside influences. Antipasti are a case in point: in the past, when hard physical work occupied country people even more than it does today, dishes such as crostini, fettunta, insalata, and panzanella were a meal in themselves, big and hearty.

Today we serve smaller versions. Black or green olives, a wisp of cured ham or beef or a few slices of salami with some raw beans, a curl of salty cheese, and a glass of local wine.

antipasti

Serve such treats with some crusty country bread to create a perfect antipasto. These recipes range from toppings for bruschetta—toasted or pan-grilled bread—to almost-raw salads, and dishes like hot, char-grilled asparagus eaten with an ooze of melting blue cheese or mozzarella. In fact many of the most interesting ingredients described on pages 8 to 13 appear to best advantage in the antipasto course, where strong flavors and interesting textures come to the fore.

You can use these dishes as the Italians do—to start a meal, to tickle the palate, provoke the appetite, then lead you into the main body of the meal. Alternatively, be generous—increase the scale and regard them as snack meals perfect and filling in themselves.

Here's an earthy, classic starter that I've enjoyed in many a Tuscan trattoria and one which is capable of many variations, as you can see from the three very different recipes below. Cheese and bacon is always a favorite topping—tomatoes and arugula is a variation on the traditional marriage of tomatoes with basil—while the chicken livers can be flavored in many ways; with sage and thyme, spices, ribbons of pancetta or prosciutto, or a tablespoon of grated fresh Parmesan cheese. Give your imagination free rein!

Bruschette e fettunte

Crusty Toasted or Char-Grilled Bread

1 small loaf country-style Italian
  bread, such as pugliese

Chicken Liver Topping:
2 tablespoons butter
2 tablespoons extra-virgin olive oil
4 garlic cloves, crushed
8 oz. chicken livers, well trimmed,
  then halved
2 tablespoons dry Marsala wine
1 tablespoon brandy or grappa
2 pinches of ground mace or cloves
  (or both)
8 sprigs of marjoram, 4 chopped and
  4 whole
sea salt and freshly ground black
  pepper

Serves 6

To make the crostini, cut thin slices from the loaf of bread, then toast or char-grill.

To make the chicken liver topping, heat the butter and oil, add the garlic and livers and sauté for 1½ to 2 minutes until golden with rosy centres (cut one to check). Pour in the wine and brandy or grappa, stir, flambé, and leave until the flames die down. Stir in the mace, cloves, chopped herbs, and seasonings to taste. Mash coarsely. Pile a mound of chicken liver paste on the toast, and top with a sprig of marjoram.

Variations:
1. Fettunta al Pomodoro con Rucola (with tomatoes and arugula)
Rub the toast with crushed garlic. Put 2 large handfuls of arugula on a plate and put the toast on top. Drizzle with 6 tablespoons extra-virgin olive oil, add sliced ripe tomatoes, season, drizzle with 4 tablespoons olive oil, add extra arugula, then serve.

2. Bruschette con Provoloncino e Pancetta (with cheese and bacon)
Slice the bread thicker than in the main recipe, then roast or char-grill on both sides, so it is hot and crusty outside yet soft in the middle. Top with provoloncino cheese (page 10) and crispy-fried strips of pancetta, then broil or char-grill until the cheese melts.

One of the most elegant Italian dishes I've ever eaten was a venison bresaola served by George Locatelli of London's Zafferano restaurant. Beef bresaola is more usual, and you could also try one of the other Italian cured meats or sausages on pages 10 and 11, cut wafer-thin. The final triumph is a drizzle of truffle oil—sold in specialty stores—or you could use olive oil infused with fresh basil leaves or lemon zest.

Bresaola al caprino

Cured Beef with Goat Cheese Salad

Slice the celery into thin, match-stick julienne strips. (If using celery root, as shown here, peel, slice into thin slices then into match-stick julienne strips.) Put in a bowl, cover with boiling water, let stand for 1 minute, drain, then refresh in ice water. Drain again and pat dry on crumpled paper towels.

Crumble the cheese and, using a fork, mash it with the oil and wine to a creamy dressing. Add the celery or celery root and toss well.

Divide the mixture between 4 serving plates, piling it into mounds. Cover with slices of bresaola, overlapping the slices in a circle around a creamy cheese center. Sprinkle with the parsley, salt, and freshly ground pepper, then drizzle with truffle oil and serve.

4 oz. celery root or 2 celery stalks

2 oz. goat cheese, such as caprino

2 tablespoons extra-virgin olive oil

2 tablespoons dry white wine

20 wafer-thin slices bresaola (cured beef), or other cured meats or salame

4 sprigs of flat-leaf parsley

4 teaspoons truffle oil

sea salt and freshly ground black pepper

Serves 4

Panzanella

At its most basic, this classic Tuscan salad is composed of crusty bread, olive oil, ripe juicy tomatoes, and seasonings. Many cooks add their own signature ingredients: balsamic or wine vinegar, salted anchovies, capers, green or black olives, chiles, roasted peppers, and fresh herbs, usually basil. Don't be shy with the bread or the oil—this is a generous, lusty dish. Salted anchovies—packed dry in large round cans, layered with coarse salt—and capers, treated the same way, can be bought from specialty stores by the *etto* (100 grams) or in individual jars. If you must substitute anchovies canned in oil or capers in brine or vinegar, drain well and proceed as above—but expect less flavor.

1½ loaves focaccia or ciabatta bread

1½ lb. ripe, red, juicy tomatoes, peeled, halved, and seeded over a small bowl to catch the juices

4 garlic cloves, crushed to a purée

8 tablespoons extra-virgin olive oil, plus extra, to serve

2 tablespoons red wine vinegar or 2 teaspoons balsamic vinegar

2 tablespoons salted capers

6 salted anchovies, filleted

12 black Italian olives

2 red, orange, or yellow bell peppers, roasted, peeled and thickly sliced

1 serrano chile, diced or sliced (optional)

4–6 sprigs of basil

Serves 4–6

Tear the bread into big chunks and toast or char-grill if preferred. Put into a large salad bowl, then add the tomato halves.

Stir the garlic, oil, and vinegar into the small bowl of reserved tomato juices.

Pour hot water over the capers and anchovies and set aside to soak for 5 minutes. Separate and fillet the anchovies and discard the bones. Drain, but reserve 2 tablespoons of the soaking liquid and add it to the tomato-juice dressing.

Add the capers, anchovies, olives, peppers, and the chile, if using, to the salad bowl. Stir the dressing and pour it all over the salad. Set aside for 30 minutes to develop the flavors, then serve with sprigs of basil and a small pitcher of extra olive oil.

There are two kinds of artichokes; the thistle-like globe artichoke and the Jerusalem artichoke—used in this salad—which is a tuber. Though they aren't related botanically, this dish can be made with either kind. In Italy there are many types of globe artichoke, often sold by variety, for example Violetti, Romani, Morellin, Spinosi, and the biggest of all, Mamare. The hearts can be bought ready-peeled and trimmed in Italian open-air markets, but outside Italy, you'll have to trim your own.

Insalata di topinambur crudi

Jerusalem Artichoke Salad

1 lb. Jerusalem artichokes

2 lemons, halved

2 tablespoons extra-virgin olive oil

4 garlic cloves, crushed

a small handful of flat-leaf
    parsley, chopped

a small handful of mint, chopped

1–2 oz. shavings of fresh
    Parmesan cheese

sea salt and freshly ground pepper

Serves 4

Scrub the artichokes, peel with a vegetable peeler, and rub with a cut lemon. Squeeze the lemon into a bowl of water. With a mandoline, stainless steel knife, or food processor with fine slicing blade, cut the artichokes into wafer-thin slices and put into the lemon water. Transfer to a colander and pour over boiling water to blanch. Drain and return to the lemon water.

When ready to serve, drain, pat dry, and arrange on a serving dish. Drizzle generously with olive oil, then squeeze the juice of the second lemon over the salad. Add the garlic, herbs, salt, and pepper, and toss until gleaming and evenly coated. Serve cool topped with slivers of Parmesan.

Variation:

If using globe artichokes, trim off the leaves and stems, slice off the tops, and rub all over with lemon. Proceed as in the main recipe.

Grigliata di asparagi

Char-Grilled Asparagus

The first time I tasted char-grilled asparagus in Italy it was a revelation—I had always poached, steamed, or microwaved it before. Char-grilling, sautéing, or barbecuing gives a full, sweet smokiness which is most appealing, though the spears discolor and wrinkle somewhat—all part of the charm. Gorgonzola combines blissfully with these flavors, and though the grappa at the end is entirely optional and idiosyncratic, it's superb.

1 lb. fresh green asparagus, wiped but not washed

2–4 tablespoons extra-virgin olive oil (see method)

3 oz. mascarpone or fontina cheese, diced

6 oz. Gorgonzola cheese, cut in 4

sea salt and lots of freshly ground black pepper

grappa, to sprinkle (optional)

Serves 4

Pre-heat a broiler, barbecue, or stove-top grill-pan until very hot. Snap off any woody ends from the asparagus (they tend to snap, accurately, at the exact spot where tough meets tender).

Drizzle a heatproof serving platter with oil, add the asparagus, and roll to coat. Remove and cook for 2 to 5 minutes on both sides (depending on age and size), then transfer to the serving platter and season to taste.

Put the mascarpone or fontina on top, then the Gorgonzola. Briefly heat under the broiler, in a hot oven, or near the barbecue until the cheeses begin to trickle deliciously at the edges. Away from the heat, sprinkle with grappa, if using, then serve with a selection of other antipasti.

Variation:

If you omit the cheese and grappa, the asparagus can be served as a vegetable accompaniment for meat, fish, or poultry.

primi piatti

first courses

These *primi piatti* or first courses have become, in some people's minds, the meal itself. Soup, gnocchi, pasta, risotto, polenta in all its guises, pizza, and piadina are probably the best-loved (and certainly the best-known) dishes of all the Italian country kitchen has to offer.

Eating in rural Italy is based on regional and seasonal differences. Many dishes cost relatively little. But what is essential is that each component be the best quality available. This way, a soup gains a wealth of flavor from a drizzle of oil and a sprinkling of herbs. Spaghetti, simply dressed with oil, garlic, and chile, has fed hungry poets and peasants for centuries— perfect fast food. Even homemade pasta is simple to make thanks to modern devices such as food processors and pasta machines, and worth the extra effort for a special occasion.

Gnocchi and polenta have ceased to be peasant's food and are now the height of fashion. Pizza and piadina, once so much the pride of country cooks, have now come to town in a big way and reflect the lusty core of the Italian kitchen. (In fact, once you've tried homemade pizza, you'll think it a completely different dish from the pizzas you buy in the big restaurant chains in other parts of the world.)

Thin, silky ravioli of homemade egg pasta with a well-seasoned filling (in this case of pumpkin, cheese, spices, and crumbs) are a great treat, and surprisingly easy to make. Mix the dough in a food processor or roll it through a hand-cranked pasta machine (see page 16 to 17). Use to make these stuffed ravioli and serve with sage leaves and a drizzle of melted butter, not oil—this recipe is from Piedmont, which is cattle country, not olive country. Use this same pasta-dough recipe to make the pasta ribbons on page 34, using the trenette cutter on your machine.

Tortelli di zucca

Pumpkin Ravioli *with Butter and Sage*

1½ cups Italian pasta flour (typo 00)
  or all-purpose flour
⅛ teaspoon salt
2 medium eggs
2 medium egg yolks
3 tablespoons semolina, for rolling

Filling and Topping:
1 lb. pumpkin, cut in 1-inch chunks
2 shallots, chopped
4 sage leaves, chopped
1 cup breadcrumbs or mashed potato
½ cup grana cheese, finely grated
¼ teaspoon grated nutmeg or mace
1 egg
6 tablespoons butter, melted
4 small sage sprigs
salt and freshly ground black pepper

Serves 4–6

To make the pasta dough, mix the first 4 ingredients in a food processor in short bursts until the mixture comes together to form a ball. Place on a surface dusted with semolina. Knead it until smooth and silky—about 3 to 4 minutes. Divide the dough into two, wrap in plastic, and chill for 30 minutes to 2 hours.

Pat one ball into a flat rectangle. Feed the dough through the rollers, following the pasta machine instructions (see pages 16–17). Cover the rolled pasta while you roll out the second ball of dough. Cover as before.

To make the filling, simmer the pumpkin, shallot, and chopped sage together in a little boiling water until tender—about 8 minutes. Drain well, then mash the flesh to a purée. Stir in the crumbs to cool the mixture, then add the cheese and nutmeg. Divide the filling into 16 to 20 portions.

To fill the pasta, unfold the dough. Put neat tablespoons of filling at 2- to 3-inch intervals on the lower half (see page 18). Beat the egg with 4 tablespoons water and paint it around the piles of filling. Fold the unfilled half of the pasta down on top and press carefully to make a good seal and exclude air bubbles. Using a fluted pasta cutter, cut into 2-inch squares, or use a 2-inch cutter to cut neat circles. Discard the trimmings.

Bring 1 or 2 large, shallow pans of water or stock to a boil. Add 2 to 3 ravioli to each pan and poach 2 to 4 minutes. (They float to the top when ready.) Drain and transfer to hot soup plates. Repeat with the remaining ravioli. Pour the melted butter over each helping, add seasonings, and sage leaves, briefly fried in butter, then serve.

Spaghetti, one of the world's best loved pastas, is available in almost every color. Italians, however, rather disapprove of colors other than white and green, though they make a special exception for *spaghetti nero*, the expensive pasta colored and flavored with squid ink. Though chiles are not very widely used in Italy, they are common in dishes from the south and from Sicily.

Spaghetti aglio e peperoncino

Spaghetti with Garlic and Chile

Cook the pasta in a large saucepan of boiling salted water, uncovered, until tender but firm (*al dente*). Drain in a colander then return it, with about ½ cup of the cooking liquid, to the saucepan.

Put the oil, red pepper flakes, garlic, and arugula, if using, in a second pan, heat briefly until aromatic, then toss the cooked spaghetti (and the reserved cooking liquid) thoroughly in this mixture, then serve.

Variation: Spaghetti alla Carbonara

My favorite version of the Roman dish of pasta with bacon and eggs is based on Elizabeth David's classic. Cook the spaghetti as in the main recipe, but do not drain. In a skillet, heat 2 tablespoons butter, add 6 oz. chopped sliced pancetta or unsmoked bacon and cook until crisp. Drain the pasta and return it to the saucepan. Add 3 lightly beaten eggs to the bacon, stir it until almost set, then transfer into the pasta. Add ½ cup grated Parmesan cheese and toss well. Serve with extra Parmesan.

12 oz. dried spaghetti

4 tablespoons extra-virgin olive oil

1 teaspoon red pepper flakes (*peperoncini*)

6–8 garlic cloves, finely sliced or chopped

2 large handfuls of fresh young arugula leaves (optional)

Serves 4–6

Trenette al pesto

Pasta Ribbons with Pesto

Pesto is the vivid green paste made from fragrant basil leaves and is the most virtuoso of all Genoese dishes. The locals believe they grow the most pungent, luxurious basil in Italy and this combination of pesto, pasta, and vegetables is traditional throughout Liguria. Pesto is also good stirred into soups, or as a topping for bruschetta, tomatoes, or chicken. Make a large quantity and use over several days. Trenette is the Ligurian form of fettuccine.

8–12 waxy new potatoes, halved

12 young green beans, topped and tailed

1 lb. homemade egg pasta, cut into
  ½-inch trenette ribbons (page 17)

1 cup pesto (recipe page 21)

freshly ground black pepper

Serves 4–6

Cook the potatoes in boiling salted water until almost tender, then add the green beans. Cook several minutes more until the beans are barely tender. Drain and divide between 4 to 6 wide soup plates.

Cook the fresh pasta in boiling salted water until it rises to the surface—about 1 to 2 minutes. Drain in a colander, retaining about ½ cup of cooking liquid. Return the pasta and water to the pan, add the vegetables and most of the pesto, and stir together.

Divide between the soup plates, sprinkle with freshly ground black pepper, and serve, together with the remaining pesto in a separate dish.

Variations:

1. Omit the vegetables and serve with a simple sauce of pesto and shavings of Parmesan.
2. Omit the vegetables and pesto and serve with the roasted tomatoes on page 69, the Salsa di pomodoro (page 21), shavings of Parmesan, and sprigs of fresh basil.
3. For a delicious and authentic Spaghetti Bolognese, omit the vegetables and pesto and serve with the Ragù on page 22.

Umbrians tend to serve a first course of soup, rather than pasta or rice. This one is a typical rustic soup, easy to make and splendidly quick except for the time taken to soak and cook the chickpeas (though you could always use ready-to-eat canned or bottled ones if you like). The large amount of parsley lifts and unites all the flavors, including the rosemary. If you're well-organized, this is the epitome of a quick and easy dish, and takes just 30 minutes. Chickpeas are also known as garbanzo beans.

Minestra di ceci

Chickpea Soup *with Potato and Parsley*

1½ cups dried chickpeas or 1¾ lb. canned or bottled chickpeas, drained

8 cups stock—meat, chicken, or vegetable—preferably homemade

a large sprig of rosemary, crushed

1 celery stalk

¼ teaspoon saffron powder or a large pinch of saffron threads (optional)

4 tablespoons extra-virgin olive oil

12 oz. potatoes (3 medium), cubed

6 garlic cloves, sliced

1 zucchini, diced

one large handful of fresh flat-leaf parsley, chopped

Serves 4–6

If using dried chickpeas, put them in a bowl, cover with cold water, and soak overnight. Drain, put in a saucepan, cover with cold water, bring to a boil, and simmer for about 2 to 2½ hours until tender (the time will depend on the age of the chickpeas). Do NOT add salt at this stage, or the beans will be tough.

When ready to cook the soup, combine the cooked chickpeas and the stock in a large saucepan and heat to simmering. Tie the sprig of rosemary to the celery stalk with string, so it will be easy to remove later. If using saffron threads, put them in a cup and cover with boiling water to soak.

Heat the oil in a skillet, add the potatoes, and sauté until golden (8 to 10 minutes). Add the garlic, sauté for another minute, then transfer the contents of the skillet into the stock. Add the zucchini and the bundle of rosemary and celery.

Simmer for 15 minutes, partly covered. If using saffron, add the powder or the saffron threads with their soaking liquid. Add half the parsley and cook for 2 minutes more. Remove the rosemary and celery, add the remaining parsley, and serve.

This is a dual-purpose risotto recipe: the first section will produce a traditional Saffron Risotto, which is served hot. If you let it cool, it can be used to make this unusual risotto cake. Both are flavored and colored with saffron: threads or strands are best, but Italian delicatessens sell very good-quality saffron powder in little sachets— just add it to a boiling stock and proceed as usual (the threads must be steeped in boiling water first). Use the best Italian risotto rice you can find—Arborio or Carnaroli are both good choices.

Risotto al salto

Italian Risotto Cake

To make the risotto, heat the butter and oil in a large saucepan, add the leek and garlic, and cook gently until softened but still pale. Add the rice and cook, stirring, for about 1 to 2 minutes until the grains are well coated with oil. Add all the saffron and its soaking water, then the stock, 1 ladle at a time, and simmer until each ladleful is absorbed before adding the next. Stir in the Parmesan and salt and serve immediately, or let cool and use to make the risotto cake.

To make the risotto cake, combine the cold rice, egg yolk, egg, and diced mozzarella in a bowl. Mix carefully. Heat the oil until very hot in a large, heavy-bottom, preferably non-stick skillet, tilting it so the oil covers the sides as well as the base.

Spoon in the rice mixture, smooth the top, and cook over moderate heat for 6 to 8 minutes or until the base is golden and there is a strong aroma. (Be sure it doesn't burn.) Put a flat saucepan lid or plate on top, then invert the skillet and plate in one quick movement. Slide the rice back in, crust up, and cook the second side until golden.

To serve, cut the cake into wedges. Serve hot or warm, sprinkled with cracked pepper, shavings of Parmesan, and leaves such as arugula, watercress, or red Belgian endive.

Saffron Risotto:

4 tablespoons salted butter

6 tablespoons extra-virgin olive oil

2 leeks, white only, finely sliced

4 garlic cloves, chopped

1⅓ cups Italian risotto rice

1 large pinch saffron threads,
    soaked in ⅓ cup boiling water for
    30 minutes

4 cups hot chicken or veal stock

2 oz. Parmesan cheese, grated or
    in shavings

sea salt, to taste

Risotto Cake:

1 lb. cooked cooled saffron risotto

1 egg yolk, beaten

1 egg, beaten

3 oz. mozzarella cheese, diced

2–3 tablespoons extra-virgin olive oil

shavings of Parmesan cheese

freshly ground black pepper

leaves such as arugula, watercress,
    or red Belgian endive

Serves 4–6

There are a number of different kinds of gnocchi, which can be rather confusing. These, made with cooked mashed potato, are the most common. Others are made with semolina, or leftover rice, and there is also a form of dried pasta that is made to resemble potato gnocchi. True gnocchi can be served with sauces, or topped with cheese and baked in the oven. All are incomparable.

Gnocchi al pomodoro

Gnocchi with Tomato Sauce

Gnocchi:

2 lb. large floury potatoes, such as Russet Burbank

2 egg yolks

1⅓ cups all-purpose flour, plus extra for rolling

pinch of salt

4 cups boiling water, beef or chicken stock, for poaching

To Serve:

2–3 cups hot Salsa de pomodoro (page 20), salsa pizzaiola (tomato-garlic sauce) or Pesto (page 21)

about 20 fresh basil leaves

1 tablespoon chopped fresh chives

freshly grated Parmesan cheese (optional)

sea salt and freshly ground black pepper

Serves 4–8

To make the gnocchi, cook the potatoes in boiling salted water until soft. Drain and either mash or press through a potato ricer into a bowl. Add the salt, then beat the egg yolks and flour into the potatoes, a little at a time, to form a smooth, slightly sticky dough.

Transfer to a well-floured board, then roll out the dough into cylinders about ½ inch in diameter. Cut each piece into sections about 1 inch long. Place each piece on the back of a fork, press down with your thumb and roll or flick the piece off the end of the fork onto the floured board, leaving grooves on one side of the gnocchi.

Pour the boiling water or stock into a saucepan, return to a boil, add the gnocchi about 20 at a time, and cook until they rise to the surface. Cook for 50 to 60 seconds more until they are cooked through, then remove with a slotted spoon to a large bowl. Repeat until all the gnocchi are done.

To serve, spoon a pool of the hot sauce into the base of 4 wide soup plates and divide the gnocchi between the plates. Sprinkle with basil leaves, chopped chives, sea salt, and pepper. Serve a small dish of grated Parmesan cheese separately if preferred.

Note: Gnocchi are sometimes made from semolina rather than potato, and cut into small cookie-shaped disks. Various sauces are suitable for gnocchi, including pesto, or tomato and garlic. They may also be covered with cheese and baked in the oven at 400°F for 35 to 40 minutes until crisp and crusty.

Serve char-grilled slabs of cooked polenta with slices of Parma ham—San Daniele is one of the best-known versions of this world-famous, delectable, rosy-pink, cured, raw, air-dried ham. Try to buy it freshly and thinly sliced from an Italian deli or gourmet store. Use other kinds of Italian *prosciutto crudo* if San Daniele is unavailable—*prosciutto di Parma* (Parma ham) is also superb.

Polenta alla griglia

Grilled Polenta *with Prosciutto*

1 lb. pre-cooked, cooled polenta
(see page 19)
olive oil, for brushing
6 slices San Daniele *prosciutto crudo* or
other good-quality Italian ham
a few salad leaves, such as arugula,
watercress, or curly endive, to serve
1 cup Parmesan cheese, shaved into
long, thin slivers
3 tablespoons first-pressing extra-virgin
olive oil, or to taste
freshly ground black pepper

Serves 6

Cut the ready-cooked polenta using a taut thread, pulling it through evenly with both hands. Alternatively, cut with a sharp knife. If the cake of polenta is very thick, cut it horizontally crosswise first to make two disks, then slice into 6 to 12 segments like a cake.

Pre-heat a cast-iron stove-top grill pan until very hot. Brush the surface of the polenta wedges with a little olive oil, then press them onto the pan and cook for 8 to 15 minutes (you must heat them thoroughly as well as crisping the crust). Using a spatula or tongs, turn over the pieces and cook the other side for another 8 to 15 minutes.

To serve, set 1 slice on each plate and drape a slice of ham over and beside it. Add a few crisp salad leaves, sprinkle with black pepper and shavings of Parmesan, then drizzle with olive oil and serve immediately.

Pizza Dough:

¾ cake fresh yeast, crumbled*

1 teaspoon sugar

1¼ cups lukewarm water

4 tablespoons extra-virgin olive oil,
    plus extra, for brushing

3⅓ cups all-purpose white flour

1½ teaspoons salt

Margherita Topping:

2 cups ripe tomatoes, skinned,
    seeded, sliced, or 1 (13 oz.) can
    Italian plum tomatoes, drained and
    chopped

2 cups sliced fresh mozzarella or
    fontina cheese

¼ cup grated Parmesan cheese
    (optional)

12 fresh basil leaves

sea salt flakes and freshly ground
    black pepper

2 tablespoons cornmeal, for dusting

olive oil, for brushing

Makes 8 small pizzas
or 1 large one

*To use active dry yeast, mix 1 package
with the flour, salt, and sugar. Add the oil
and water and proceed with the recipe.

The pizza, one of the glories of Neapolitan cooking, has migrated around the world. In 1889, King Umberto and Queen Margherita arrived in Naples. A local pizza-maker, Don Raffaele, took a selection of pizzas to the palace. The Queen chose the red, white, and green one with tomatoes, mozzarella, and fresh basil leaves to match the new Italian flag—and this pizza was named in her honor.

La pizza margherita

If using fresh yeast, put it in a bowl, add the sugar and water, let froth for 5 to 10 minutes, then stir in the oil. Put the flour and salt in a large mixing bowl. Using a wooden spoon, beat in the yeast mixture to make a soft, sticky dough. Place on a lightly floured surface and knead for 5 to 8 minutes, or until soft and satiny.

Wash and dry the bowl and rub with a little oil. Roll the ball of dough in the bowl to coat with oil, then cover the bowl with plastic and let the dough rise in a warm place for 35 to 50 minutes or until doubled in size.

Heat a pizza stone or baking tray in the oven at 425°F for 30 to 40 minutes, and prepare the topping ingredients.

Place the dough on a floured work surface, punch it down with your fist and divide into 8, or leave whole. Pat and pull the dough into disk shapes. Drop onto the cornmeal, then onto the baking tray or stone. Sprinkle with the tomatoes, cheese, basil, and seasonings.

Slide the baking tray or stone into the top third of the oven. Bake for 25 to 35 minutes if large, and 15 to 20 minutes if small (2 or 3 at a time). Cook until crusty and aromatic, rub or brush a film of extra oil around the rim for a professional finish, then serve.

Variations: Pizza Bianca
Top with 6 to 8 tablespoons extra-virgin olive oil, 12 sliced garlic cloves, 3 tablespoons fresh rosemary, 12 sliced olives, 1 teaspoon sea salt, and lots of freshly ground pepper.

Pizza alla Siciliana
Top with 6 tablespoons Salsa di pomodoro (page 20), 6 anchovy fillets, 2 oz. sliced provolone or caciocavallo cheese (page 18), 1 (14 oz.) can artichoke hearts, drained, 2 teaspoons dried oregano, salt, and pepper. Add ½ cup chopped prosciutto ham and ½ cup diced mozzarella cheese 5 minutes before the end of cooking time.

Piadina

Piadina Bread *with Mushrooms and Cheese*

Piadina, also known as focaccia, is the typical unleavened flatbread of the Romagna area. It helps to have a *testo* (terra-cotta baking stone), which distributes heat evenly like a true baker's oven and helps to make the bread crisp and crusty. Round, square, or rectangular, these stones are sold in specialist cooking equipment stores, but you could also use a heavy skillet or baking tray instead. Pre-heat it for 30 minutes at 400°F and sprinkle with polenta (never oil) before adding the dough.

3⅓ cups all-purpose flour
2 tablespoons butter, melted
sea salt, to taste
about 1 cup plus 1 tablespoon warm
  water (at blood heat)
about 2 cups cornmeal, to stop sticking

Topping:
2 whole mozzarella (4 oz. each)
4 oz. porcini mushrooms, bottled in oil
2 teaspoons fresh rosemary or oregano

Serves 4 or 6

Put the flour, butter, salt, and about half the water in a food processor or electric mixer and mix to a soft dough, drizzling in more water as needed. Pre-heat the baking stone or cast-iron skillet on the top shelf of the oven at 400°F for 30 minutes.

Hand-knead the dough on a floured work surface for 4 to 5 minutes. Transfer to a bowl, cover with plastic or a cloth, and let stand in a warm place for 30 minutes. Divide into 4 to 6 balls, each about the size of a small apple. Pat out the dough, then roll into disks 6- to 7-inch diameter.

Scatter cornmeal over the baking stone or skillet and slap on the dough. Cook for several minutes until hot, bubbling, and aromatic, then flip over the bread using tongs or a spatula. Cook 2 to 3 minutes longer until browned.*

Slice the mozzarella and porcini and divide between the piadine. Sprinkle with salt and herbs and serve hot. Return them to the oven for a few minutes to melt the cheese.

*****Note:** You can also brown it quickly under a preheated broiler, or over a gas flame.

Fish, poultry, game, and meat are the dishes which promote pride and passion in the heart of every Italian cook. Here their talents have a real chance to shine!

A vast selection of sparkling-fresh fish and seafood is caught in lakes and rivers as well as the Mediterranean, and fish is served in many ways—wrapped in paper, crisped quickly in olive oil with herbs or spices, oven-baked, barbecued, sautéed, or broiled with a dash of wine, spice, citrus, or herbs.

Wildlife still thrives in Italy's forests, hillsides, and marshes, and game birds—wrapped in prosciutto, roasted quickly, and served on a bed of polenta—are favorite dishes. The meat of the wild boar or *cinghiale* is a prized ingredient, appearing roasted, or in pâtés and ragùs.

secondi piatti

second courses

On a more domesticated note, the subtle taste of the familiar chicken or special-occasion duck is enlivened by the assertive flavors of Italian herbs and spices.

Huge and splendid beefsteaks, often from the enormous white Chianina cattle of Tuscany, produce the legendary *bistecca fiorentina*, one of the world's great beef dishes. Other cuts are pan-fried, then deglazed with a sticky Italian dessert wine or broiled and sliced onto a bed of bitter arugula leaves. Veal, too, is a favorite meat in Italy, and veal dishes such as *saltimbocca*—"jump in the mouth"—are justly famous.

Red snapper (red mullet in Italy) is cooked to perfection nestling in a bed of trevise (Italian long-leafed red chicory) with orange-flavored oil and onion. Each serving is cooked as an individual package, to be unwrapped and savored at the table. No red-leafed chicory? Use a red-leafed lettuce (red cabbage is not delicate enough). Along the coast, fish is sometimes also wrapped in fresh grape leaves or fig leaves instead (paper is too fragile to cook over embers), and sometimes in foil. This dish tastes great, whichever way you cook it.

Triglia al cartoccio

Red Snapper in a Package

4 American red snapper, 10 oz. each, cleaned, scaled, and filleted

the zest and juice of 1 orange

1 red onion, sliced into rings

1–2 heads trevise (red Italian chicory) or radicchio

2 tablespoons extra-virgin olive oil

2 garlic cloves, chopped

freshly ground salt and black pepper

4 pieces parchment paper, about 12 inches square

Serves 4

Pre-heat the oven to 450°F and put one of the racks towards the top of the oven to heat.

Put the fillets, skin side up, into a shallow non-reactive dish with the orange zest and juice and onions. Put several leaves of trevise at the center of each paper square. Heat the oil and garlic gently until the garlic smells aromatic. Press the pairs of fillets together with some onion and zest between. Set each pair on a leaf bed. Pour over a little of the juice and a portion of the oil and garlic mixture.

Fold the 2 long sides of the paper together in a concertina-like fold, then twist the 2 short ends closed and tuck them underneath. Continue until all the packages are made. Using a spatula, lift the packages onto a large shallow roasting pan or baking tray—they should not touch.

Bake in the preheated oven for 8 to 12 minutes or until the packages have puffed up a little and, when tested, the flesh is firm and white (open one to see). Serve the packages whole—your guests can unwrap them and enjoy the wonderful scent.

A typical dish, served in seaside restaurants around Capri and other seaside resorts, is *calamaretti*, or tiny whole squid. Under 2 inches long, these are delicious, charming, and unbelievably sweet and succulent. Small to medium tender squid, about 5 to 6 inches long, are also suitable and can be stuffed, as here—they are much easier to buy, and are often sold frozen.

Calamari ripieni fritti

Stuffed Fried Squid

Put all the stuffing ingredients into a food processor and process, in bursts, to a crumbly consistency. (Do not over-process until dense.)

Pat the squid dry with paper towels. Pull off the head section below the eyes. Discard the body contents, the cellophane-like quill, and the eye section, but keep the tentacles. Continue until all are prepared. Pack a little stuffing loosely into the body of each squid. Secure with a wooden toothpick, at an angle. Pat the squid dry again on paper towels. Dust generously in the flour.

Pour the oil in to a skillet to a depth of about ½ inch and heat until very hot. Add about 6 to 8 squid and tentacles at a time. Sauté for a very short time, about 50 to 60 seconds per side or until golden and aromatic and the flesh is firm and opaquely white. Turn and repeat on the second side. Using a slotted spoon, remove and drain on crumpled paper towels. Keep hot in the oven at 400°F while you cook the remainder, which should also be kept in the oven for 5 minutes. Serve with lemon wedges.

Note: I always leave the pretty purple skin on the squid—it looks and tastes wonderful.

1 lb. squid, about 5–6 inches long, fresh or frozen and defrosted
all-purpose flour, for dusting
olive oil, for cooking
lemon wedges, to serve

Herb Stuffing:
4 tablespoons chopped parsley
4 tablespoons torn basil leaves
4 tablespoons chopped rosemary
2 slices stale country bread, crumbled
⅓ cup grated Parmesan
salt and freshly ground pepper

Serves 4

Tuna is a delicious, dense, meaty fish which demands strong but vivid treatment. In ports around the Calabrian coast many restaurants offer delicious and interesting dishes using tuna. This recipe, though eminently simple, is absolutely effortless, tasty, and a treat. It can also be applied to swordfish, and to large, raw unpeeled shrimp—*gamberi*—with excellent results.

Tonno alla griglia

Char-Grilled Tuna

1 orange or large lemon, halved

4 tuna steaks, about ½ inch thick

2 teaspoons freshly puréed garlic

freshly ground black pepper

16 fresh sage leaves, half chopped,
   half whole

8 tablespoons extra-virgin olive oil

Serves 4

Using a sharp knife, remove and discard the rind and pith from the orange or lemon. Cut between the pith sections to separate pith-free segments. (Keep the juice-filled membranes to squeeze over the fish.) Reserve the segments for serving.

Pat the tuna steaks dry on paper towels. Mash together the garlic, pepper, and chopped sage leaves. Cut 2 slashes, at an angle, on one side of each steak, to about ⅔ thickness. Push a little of the herb seasoning into each slash. Drizzle the steaks with 2 tablespoons oil and set aside to develop the flavors while you heat the broiler, barbecue, or stove-stop grill pan until very hot.

Lift the prepared fish onto the rack or pan. Cook quickly so that the outside sizzles but the inside remains rare. Turn the fish over after 1 minute, using tongs or spatula, then cook the second side.

Meanwhile heat the remaining oil until very hot, throw in the whole sage leaves (they will crisp) and remove from the heat. Serve the fish with hot oil, the crisp sage leaves, a squeeze of orange or lemon juice and 1 to 2 segments of the citrus fruit on top.

Variation: Char-Grilled Shrimp

Substitute 12 to 16 large shrimp for the tuna, and fresh marjoram or oregano for the sage leaves (but do not crisp in the hot oil). Slash the shrimp through the shell and down the length of the curved back. Pull out and discard the thin black thread. Stuff each shrimp with some of the garlic mixture. Barbecue, broil, or char-grill, adapting the time until all shrimp are firmly white and opaque right through, with red shells.

In this recipe quail are first roasted, then flambéed with grappa, the famously distinctive, delicious Italian *eau de vie*—a fiery liquor made from the debris (lees) left from grapes after pressing. It can be young and fierce, or aged in wood to a mellow, smoky state. A robust red wine is also used to deglaze the pan and produce a flavorful, colorful sauce. Quail is usually classed as game and, though this bird is mostly farmed these days, Italians have always been very fond of game, both feathered and furred.

Quaglie arrosto con polenta

Roast Quail on a Bed of Polenta

4 prepared quail*

4 garlic cloves, dry-sautéed for about
   3–5 minutes until golden

4 sprigs of sage

4 sprigs of thyme

24 black olives or black grapes

2 slices prosciutto or smoked bacon,
   halved crosswise

6 tablespoons grappa or brandy

4 tablespoons robust red Italian wine

salt and freshly ground pepper

1 quantity wet polenta (page 19),
   to serve

Serves 4

* If serving the quail without polenta, double
the quantity of quail, herbs and bacon.

Season the birds well, inside and out. Stuff with the garlic, half the herbs, and 12 olives or grapes. Wrap in pieces of prosciutto and set them in a large flameproof roasting pan, breast side down. Put the remaining herbs, and olives or grapes under and around the birds.

Roast in a preheated oven at 425°F for 18 to 25 minutes. Using tongs, turn the birds over. Reduce the heat to 400°F and continue roasting 15 minutes longer if necessary, or until golden, aromatic, and crisp.

Set the pan on top of the stove over a high heat. Pour half the grappa over the birds and carefully light it with a long match, then stand back. When the flames die down, add the wine and the rest of the grappa. Scrape up the sediment from the pan and let the gravy bubble over medium heat until flavorful and a little reduced.

Remove the birds, cover them with foil, and let them stand in a warm place for 5 minutes. Serve on a bed of wet polenta, with the pan juices poured over and around.

Variations:

1. To cook chicken, roast for 20 minutes per pound at 425°F, then reduce the heat and roast for a further 20 minutes. Proceed as in the main recipe.

2. To serve on a bed of lentils, cook 1¼ cups Castelluccio lentils and 2 garlic cloves in 3 cups unsalted water for 20 to 25 minutes or until tender. Drain, stir in 4 tablespoons extra-virgin olive oil, salt, and pepper and use instead of the bed of polenta.

3. Poach pre-cooked zampone or cotechino in herb-flavored water for 20 to 35 minutes until heated through, then slice and serve on a bed of polenta or lentils.

Polpette are made all over Italy using finely minced lamb, beef, veal, or pork with whatever accents suit them best: cheese, herbs, sausage, capers, citrus zest, pignoli nuts, chiles, and even anchovy. In Sicily lemon leaves are common, but if this is not the case in your area, substitute grated or finely sliced lemon zest. Before cooking, either roll the meatballs in grated zest, or insert sliced zest.

Polpette al limone

Meatballs with Lemon

Purea di patate
Potato Mash *with Garlic*

3 lb. yellow, waxy potatoes, peeled

2 heads garlic, top ½ inch discarded

6–8 tablespoons extra-virgin olive oil

½ teaspoon saffron threads or
    ¼ teaspoon saffron powder
    (optional)

salt and freshly ground black pepper

Serves 4–6

Boil the potatoes and garlic in salted water, covered, for 20–25 minutes or until soft. Drain. Return both to the hot saucepan, heat turned off. Heat the oil in a second pan, add the saffron threads ground with salt, or the saffron powder, if using. Squeeze out the garlic pulp and add to the oil. Add the potatoes and mash well. When smooth, creamy, and evenly gold, season with freshly ground black pepper and serve.

1 lb. twice-minced lean lamb

8 oz. *luganega* or other coarse Italian
    sausage, removed from its casing

2 slices stale Italian bread (about 3 oz.)

beef stock or water, for dipping bread

1 egg, beaten

1 small bunch flat-leaf parsley, chopped

4 garlic cloves, chopped

½ teaspoon ground allspice, mace, or
    nutmeg

1 teaspoon sea salt

6 tablespoons grated Parmesan cheese

freshly ground black pepper

24 fresh lemon leaves (optional)

juice and zest of 1 lemon

24 toothpicks

6–8 tablespoons olive oil, for cooking

stock, wine, or water, to deglaze the pan

Serves 4

Mix the lamb and sausage meat thoroughly together with a wooden spoon. Soak the bread in the stock or water or 2 minutes then squeeze dry and crumble in with the meats. Add the beaten egg, parsley, garlic, spice, salt, cheese, and pepper. Beat and knead to a smooth paste. Using wet (or oiled) hands, divide into 24 balls. Pinch and squeeze to make them compact, then flatten slightly. If using leaves, fasten one onto each ball with a toothpick. Alternatively, roll the balls in grated lemon zest or insert a strip of zest.

Heat half the oil, in a large skillet. Sauté half of the *polpette*, for 2 to 3 minutes each side, until golden, firm, and aromatic. Remove from the pan, keep hot and repeat with the remaining oil and polpette. Squeeze the juice of the lemon into the pan and add a little stock, wine, or water to the pan to dissolve the pan sediment. Pour the pan juices over the *polpette* and serve.

The Italian word *saltimbocca* means "to jump in the mouth" and these tasty little bites of veal do just that—but not for long—they are eaten so quickly. In some regions of Italy, such as Brescia and Lombardy, these are traditionally made with veal and sometimes pork, while turkey is a new favorite. The secret is to pound the meat until very thin, so cooking is almost instantaneous. Deglaze the pan using vermouth or Marsala, and serve quickly, perhaps with herbed tagliatelle and a glass of fruity Italian red wine.

Saltimbocca

Veal Escalopes *with Ham, Sage, and Cheese*

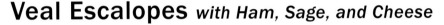

12 oz. veal escalopes

16 fresh sage leaves

8 thin slices *prosciutto crudo* (about

   3 oz.), halved crosswise

4 tablespoons sweet butter

1 tablespoons olive oil

3 oz. mozzarella cheese, thinly sliced

6 tablespoons dry Italian vermouth or dry

   Marsala wine

freshly ground black pepper

Serves 4

Using a meat mallet or rolling pin, beat out the escalopes between 2 sheets of thick plastic or parchment paper until almost doubled in size. Cut into 8 approximately even portions. Put 1 sage leaf and ½ slice of prosciutto on each. Secure with a toothpick. Season well with pepper.

   Heat the butter and oil in a heavy-based skillet. Add the *saltimbocca* to the pan, ham-side down, leaving a little room around each one, so they don't touch. Sauté for about 1½ minutes each side, pressing down to help make contact with the hot skillet.

   Turn the escalopes ham-side up. Remove the sticks. Set a slice of mozzarella and another sage leaf on top. Cover and cook again until the cheese trickles and melts. Remove from the skillet and keep them warm while you cook the remaining *saltimbocca*.

   Remove all the pieces from the skillet and deglaze with vermouth or Marsala. Stir, quickly pour the sauce over the *saltimbocca*, and serve hot.

Many Italians maintain that well-cooked ossobuco can be eaten with a spoon. *Oss bus* in Milanese dialect means "bone with a hole"—inside the hole is the creamy bone marrow, the choicest part of the dish. Get your butcher to cut clean chunks of the hind shin, about 2 inches thick, then tie up the pieces with string so the marrow doesn't accidentally fall out during cooking. This authentic version doesn't contain tomatoes. Instead, it is flavored with anchovy and sprinkled with gremolata, made from lemon zest, parsley, and garlic.

Ossobuco alla milanese

Braised Veal Shanks *with Gremolata*

8 pieces shin of veal, 2 inches thick (tied
   up with string to keep in the marrow)

⅓ cup all-purpose flour

6 tablespoons extra-virgin olive oil

4 tablespoons unsalted butter

2 onions, sliced into rings

2 carrots, diced or sliced

2 celery sticks, diced or sliced

6 salted or 8 canned anchovies, chopped

2 cups medium white wine

1 cup veal, beef, or chicken stock

a small bunch of herbs, such as parsley,
   thyme, bay, and lovage (if available)
   tied together

freshly ground salt and black pepper

Gremolata (topping):

finely grated zest of ½ lemon

a small bunch of flat-leaf parsley, chopped

2 garlic cloves, puréed

Serves 4–6

Choose a flameproof casserole dish or shallow saucepan so the meat will fit snugly. Dust the meat with the flour on both sides. Heat the oil in the casserole and brown the meat for 5 minutes on each side, turning carefully.

Heat the butter in a skillet and brown the onions, carrots, and celery. Mash in the anchovies. Add the wine and let bubble for 2 minutes.

Lift up the meat and, using a slotted spoon, add half the vegetable-anchovy mixture. Put the veal on top and pour over the remaining vegetable-anchovy mixture. Trickle the stock down the sides until the meat is nearly covered, then add the bunch of herbs.

Bring to a boil, cover, reduce the heat to very low, and simmer for 1½ to 2 hours on top of the stove, or in a pre-heated oven at 300°F for 2½ hours.

To make the gremolata, mix the lemon zest, parsley, and garlic together.

When the meat is tender, cut the string and serve the pieces carefully in heated soup plates. Spoon some of the sauce over each helping, then add the gremolata on top.

The traditional accompaniment for ossobuco is Saffron Risotto (page 38) but Saffron Mash (page 56) or Polenta (page 19) are also good.

Variation:

This recipe can also be used with lamb shanks rather than ossobuco. Allow 1 to 2 shanks per person, depending on size.

3 lb. boned leg of pork, rolled out flat,
   skin scored at ½-inch intervals
sea salt
8–12 branches of rosemary
8 garlic cloves, halved lengthwise
2 teaspoons black peppercorns,
   coarsely ground
2–3 teaspoons dried oregano
3–4 tablespoons clear honey

Anchovy and Caper Gravy:
6 canned anchovies, mashed,
   or 3 salted anchovies, filleted
   and chopped
½ cup meat stock
½ cup robust red wine
2 teaspoons balsamic vinegar
2–3 teaspoons tiny capers packed in
   salt, rinsed

Serves 8

Maiale arrosto

Crunchy Roast Pork

Roast suckling pig—golden succulent and milk-tender—is sold at the crossroads and marketplaces throughout Tuscany, and is the ultimate takeout food. It has a grand and ancient lineage, but most of us would find this recipe for a boned-out section of a leg of pork, covered in golden, crisped crackling, easier to deal with. This special dish, with its superb sweet flavors and intense sharp gravy, is excellent for large family gatherings and celebrations.

Put the pork, skin side up, in a colander standing in a sink. Pour boiling water over the meat to set, firm, and dehydrate the skin so it will crackle more quickly.

Pat the meat dry with paper towels, then set it flat in a large roasting pan. Rub generously with a handful of sea salt pushing it into the slashes. Insert the rosemary and garlic, scatter with the pepper and oregano, then drizzle with a fine network of honey.

Cook, uncovered, in a preheated oven at 475°F for about 20 to 25 minutes or until the skin has started to sizzle and color. Reduce the heat to 350°F and roast, uncovered, basting occasionally for another 1¼ to 1½ hours until the meat is golden, aromatic, and crackling crisp. Check the interior using a meat thermometer: it should register 195°F—if necessary roast a little longer.

Remove the meat to a serving dish, cover, and set aside in a warm place.

To make the gravy, pour off excess fat from the pan and place over a medium heat. Mash the anchovies into the pan juices, then pour in the stock, wine, and vinegar. Stir well, then boil for 5 minutes more, stirring often, until reduced by about half. Add the capers, and cook for 2 minutes.

To serve, cut the pork into thick slices, and serve with pieces of crackling and a spoonful of the anchovy and caper gravy.

Note: The crackling becomes very dark, so if you would prefer it lighter, use only half the honey at the beginning, and add the remainder 1 hour later.

Tagliata alla rucola

Sliced Beef on a Bed of Arugula

The handsome white Chianina cattle from the valley of the same name in Tuscany are admired for the champion beef they yield. Visitors to Tuscany are often amazed by its delicious succulence. Use the best-quality beef available in your local area to produce this tender, char-grilled, rare-cooked steak teamed with bitter arugula leaves. Arugula has been popular in Italy since Roman times. When young and fresh it is good in salads: older leaves can be used in pasta sauces, or wilted in oil and served as a vegetable.

6 tablespoons extra-virgin olive oil

1 aged rump steak (2 lb.), 1-inch thick

4 garlic cloves, crushed

2 tablespoons red wine

2 teaspoons balsamic vinegar

4 large handfuls baby arugula, chilled

1 red onion, sliced into fine rings

a small handful of fresh chives, parsley,
    or chervil (or a combination)

salt and freshly ground black pepper

Serves 4

Rub 1 tablespoon of the oil into the steak together with the garlic. Let stand up to 1 hour to develop the flavors. Mix the remaining oil in a bowl with the red wine, the balsamic vinegar, salt, and pepper to make a dressing.

Heat a barbecue, broiler, or stove-top grill-pan until very hot. Put the steak diagonally on the surface and let sizzle for 2 minutes, pressing down occasionally (the heat must be intense). Turn the steak over and cook for 2 minutes more or until aromatic and firm though still rare. Remove the pan from the heat, cover with foil, and set aside in a warm place for 2 minutes.

Toss the arugula, onion, and herbs in half the dressing and divide between 4 plates. Carve the steak into thin slices, and keep all the juices. Pile the meat on top of the greens, stir the steak juices into the remaining dressing, then drizzle over each serving. Serve with crusty country bread.

Note: Baby spinach, chicory, or watercress may be used instead of arugula.

contorni

vegetables and salads

Vegetables and salads are treated with respect in Italy. These dishes, which give proper balance to a meal, are some of the most delicious imaginable. These days many Italian vegetables, such as the long, dark green cabbage *cavolo nero,* are sold even in supermarkets. Bundles of asparagus, baskets of artichokes, boxes of bell peppers, bunches of arugula, radicchio, and wild greens grace even the most humble market stalls around the world, as well as in Italy. *Misticanza* is the Roman name for a delicious combination of colorful baby leafy greens, wild leaves, and salad herbs. Unfortunately, these aren't available outside Italy, but many other mixtures are.

Mashed potato is common in many cuisines, but made the Italian way with garlic, saffron, and oil it really is bliss. Slow-cooked white cannellini beans, dressed with good oil and served in dozens of ways, are a staple of the Italian kitchen and can stand as a meal in their own right, as do the best Italian grey-green lentils from the beautiful lentil-growing region around Castelluccio in Umbria.

Sadly, these days we are all too often shocked at the idea of a deep-fried vegetable, but if done well and cooked correctly, the batter does not soak up the oil: classic Italian *fritti* are superb and delicate—so fry it and try it! Make sure all the fleshy vegetables are sliced very thinly, or they will not cook through in the short cooking time. Leafy vegetables and herbs are perfect cooked whole.

Fritto misto di verdure

Mixed Deep-Fried Vegetables

1 whole eggplant

2 whole zucchini

4 asparagus stalks, trimmed

1 head of fennel, trimmed

8 small spinach leaves, stemmed

16 arugula leaves

sprigs of parsley or basil

2 red bell peppers, seeded, cut into
  2–inch strips or thick rings

2–3 lemons, halved, to serve

peanut, sunflower, or olive oil,
  for frying

Batter:

1 cup plus 1 tablespoon all-purpose
  flour

½ teaspoon salt

4 tablespoons olive oil

about 1½ cups hot water

4 egg whites

2 lemons, halved

freshly ground black pepper

Serves 4–6

To make the batter, sift the flour and salt into a bowl. Mix the oil and water together in a jug and pour into the bowl, beating to create a gold, creamy mixture. Let stand for about 30 minutes to 2 hours.

Meanwhile, cut the eggplant and zucchini lengthwise into thin slices. Pat dry with paper towels. Leave the asparagus whole, slice the fennel lengthwise into narrow strips, and slice the bell peppers into 2-inch strips or thick rings.

Using an electric or hand-held rotary beater, beat the egg whites until soft peaks form. Fold this mixture into the batter.

Fill a large saucepan or wok one-third full with the oil and heat to 340°F or until a ½-inch cube of bread browns in 30 seconds.

Using tongs, dip each vegetable slice first into the frothy batter, then into the hot oil. Cook in batches until golden and aromatic, about 3 to 4 minutes all together, turning over after 1 minute. Sprinkle with freshly ground black pepper and serve with the lemon halves.

Beans—cannellini, borlotti (also called *fagioli scritti*), *fave* (fava beans), *ceci* (chickpeas), and flageolets—are an Italian speciality. The secret is to soak them first, then drain and cook in fresh water—never add salt until after they're cooked. Dried beans—especially red kidney beans—should be boiled rapidly for about 10 minutes at the beginning of a recipe. Serve beans hot, warm, or cool, but never chilled.

Cannellini con pomodori

White Beans *with Roasted Tomatoes*

Soak the beans in a bowl of warm water for 4 hours or overnight. Drain and rinse, transfer to a saucepan, and cover with boiling water to twice their depth. Add the garlic and thyme. Bring to a boil, boil hard for 10 minutes, reduce the heat, skim off any scum, then partly cover, and simmer for 1 to 1½ hours or until tender.

While the beans are cooking, seed the tomato halves and put them upright on a foil-lined oven rack. Sprinkle with the salt, pepper, sugar, and half the oil. Roast in a preheated oven at 500°F until caramelized. Set aside to stir into the beans at serving time. Alternatively, the tomatoes can be broiled or char-grilled.

Drain the beans, reserving about ½ cup of liquid. Add the vinegar, remaining oil, salt, pepper, and tomatoes. Stir in the reserved liquid and serve.

2 cups dried cannellini beans (white kidney beans) or borlotti beans

2 garlic cloves, unpeeled

a small bunch of thyme sprigs

4 garlic cloves, crushed to a purée

4 plum tomatoes, halved lengthwise

2 teaspoons sugar

6 tablespoons extra-virgin olive oil

2 tablespoons red wine vinegar

salt and freshly ground black pepper

Serves 6

Variation:

This recipe can also be made with 2 cups Castelluccio or Puy lentils, cooked for about 20 to 35 minutes in unsalted water. No pre-soaking is required.

My first visit to Rome's Campo dei Fiori was a delight, with superb vegetables, many prepared to order on the spot by skilled market sellers. Puntarelle, a coiled wild chicory often eaten raw, is rarely available elsewhere. I substitute scallions, cut lengthwise into fine shreds then curled in ice water. Combine crisp and soft leaves, herbs, one or two bitter or distinctive flavors like arugula, cress, or endive, and some delicate ones like lamb's lettuce.

Insalata verde

Green Salad

1 large or 2 small romaine
  lettuces, leaves torn
1 head Belgian endive, separated
1 soft round lettuce or ½ head
  curly endive (frisée), torn
1 handful of lamb's lettuce
1 handful of arugula or
  watercress, leaves torn
½ head other Italian greens, such
  as escarole
2 scallions, sliced lengthwise,
  then soaked in ice water to curl

fresh herbs such as chives, chervil,
  basil, borage, or parsley, torn or
  scissor-cut
2 garlic cloves, crushed to a pulp
  with salt and pepper
8 tablespoons extra-virgin olive oil
a few drops of balsamic vinegar
1 tablespoon red wine vinegar
⅓ cup grana or Parmesan cheese,
  cut into long slivers (optional)

Serves 6–8

Put all the leaves, scallions, and herbs in a large salad bowl. Mix the crushed garlic, oil, and both vinegars, then drizzle over the salad. Toss 20 to 30 times and serve topped with cheese shavings, if using.

Cavolo nero in agrodolce

Cabbage in Sweet-Sour Sauce

The long leaves of *cavolo nero* are not so much black, as its name implies, but deep, rich green. They are seen more and more in markets, specialty stores, and even supermarkets. According to experts, the plants don't reach their best until they have felt the first frost—so look out for them to make a fall treat. This dish is an excellent accompaniment to roasts and spit-cooked birds and game, especially venison and wild boar.

4 tablespoons virgin olive oil

2 onions, sliced into rings

2 garlic cloves, crushed

1 lb. *cavolo nero* or Savoy cabbage, cut in 1-inch slices

1 teaspoon salt, or 2 canned anchovies, chopped

24 ripe green or black grapes

2 tablespoons seedless raisins

8 juniper berries (optional)

2 tablespoons honey

2 tablespoons red wine vinegar

4 tablespoons red wine

2 tablespoons pignoli nuts

Serves 4–6

Heat the oil, onion, and garlic in a skillet until wilted. Lift half the mixture into a saucepan. Add the *cavolo nero* and about 4 tablespoons of water—enough barely to cover the bottom of the pan. Add the salt or anchovies, cover the saucepan and bring to the boil. Reduce the heat and cook for 10 minutes or until tender.

Meanwhile, add the grapes, currants or raisins, juniper berries if using, honey, vinegar, wine, and pignolis to the remaining oil-onion-garlic mixture. Shake over the heat until the grapes look softened but are still whole and the dried fruits are plump (about 5 minutes). Reduce the heat.

When the cabbage is tender, stir in the sweet-sour sauce, cook together briefly and serve.

Though the dessert or *dolci* list is one of the glories of Italian restaurants around the world, Italians don't usually eat sweet things after lunch or dinner. Instead, they prefer to satisfy their sugar cravings in the morning. As in other parts of Europe, wonderful sweet pastries are served with endless cups of some of the world's greatest coffee brews. Italians enjoy sweet little mouthfuls with milky, frothy coffee until midday, but nobody with any pride would take anything but intense black espresso any later in the day. In fact, coffee-drinking in Italy is an art all its own, and if you care to, you could spend a lifetime studying it.

A cake or torta like the one on the next page, perhaps with a dollop of mascarpone, is the sort of thing that would be served with coffee for breakfast, and also as a late-night nibble with a

dolci

sweet things

glass of fiery spirit. Its flavors of almonds, orange flower water, and citrus reflect its Saracen origins—an influence common all around the Mediterranean. You can serve it as a dessert at the end of a meal, or as the Italians would, for breakfast, or with morning coffee or afternoon tea.

Elegant desserts, such as *panna cotta*, frothy *zabaione*, and figs roasted with honey—Italian to the core—have become the sort of stylish food which can be served in *trattorie* from Trieste to Tennessee and have become party pieces for the home cook.

Panna cotta is currently all the rage around the world, but it has never gone out of fashion in its homeland. It follows a time-honored formula and is easy to prepare. Keep it minimally sweet. Roasted or broiled figs and a pool of crème anglaise can be served with it—though purists would no doubt be scandalized. It is important that panna cotta is delicate, soft and not too firm. Serve it in its pot, or turned out. Italian figs—dripping with ripe, honeyed sweetness—give this dish a properly Roman touch.

Panna cotta con fichi al forno

Cream Custard with Roasted Figs

3–4 tablespoons superfine sugar

1 cup heavy cream

1 vanilla bean, slit

8 oz. mascarpone cheese

1½ level teaspoons gelatin granules

2 tablespoons sweet dessert wine,
   Marsala wine, or dark rum

1 teaspoon almond oil or other mild
   oil, for brushing the pots

4 ripe figs

2 tablespoons clear honey, for drizzling

fennel seeds (optional)

To serve (optional):

crème anglaise

crisp cookies, such as cantuccini
   or amaretti

Serves 4–6

Simmer the sugar, cream, and vanilla bean for 5 to 8 minutes, stirring occasionally to extract the tiny black seeds. Remove, scrape clean, wash, and dry the vanilla bean and store it in a bottle of sugar, rum, or brandy for future use.

Beat the mascarpone into the hot cream away from the heat. Stir the gelatin into the wine or liquor. Leave it to swell (hydrate) then stand it over boiling water for several minutes until melted and dissolved. (Alternatively do this in a heatproof cup in the microwave: 20 seconds on HIGH for an 800 watt machine.)

Lightly oil 4 to 6 ramekins, or small china or glass pots if serving in the pot. Pour the custard into the containers. Chill for 2 hours (or longer) or until set. Serve in the pot or turn them out by running a knife blade around the sides of the ramekins.

Cut the figs in quarters lengthwise, drizzle with honey, and top with fennel seeds, if using. Broil under a hot broiler or roast in a preheated oven at 500°F until bubbling-hot, aromatic, and tender.

Serve with the panna cotta and crème anglaise or little cookies, if using.

Variations:

1. Substitute 1 crushed cinnamon stick for the vanilla bean.
2. Use 8 drops almond extract, instead of the vanilla bean.
3. Add 1 oz. dark chocolate, chopped, to the cream. Melt. Dust with cocoa and serve.
4. Add 2 teaspoons orange zest plus 8 drops of orange flower water to the mixture.

Before the discovery of corn in the Americas, polenta was made from a native European grain called spelt. It is now instantly recognizable from its glorious corn-gold color. That color makes this cake beautiful as well as delicious—perfect for parties or every day, served plain, or with indulgent additions such as whipped mascarpone, sour cream, Marsala, Vin Santo, or a fiery eau de vie.

Torta di polenta

Polenta Cake *with Lemon and Almonds*

Sift the first 3 ingredients into a bowl. Using an electric hand-held whisk, rotary beater, or balloon whisk, beat the butter in a second bowl until pale. Gradually beat in the sugar until the mixture is creamy and light, then beat in the eggs, one after another.

Stir in the vanilla and almond extracts, half the lemon zest and half the juice, then firmly fold in the dry ingredients until thoroughly mixed. Smooth into the prepared cake pan and scatter the remaining lemon zest on top.

Cook in a preheated oven at 325°F for 35 to 45 minutes or until a skewer pushed into the center comes out clean and the sides have shrunk in slightly.

Pour over the remaining lemon juice and serve the cake warm, in wedges. Whipped mascarpone, sour cream, or even ice cream make delicious accompaniments, together with a glass of Marsala, eau de vie, or Vin Santo.

Variation:

Drizzle about ½ cup sweet wine or spirit, such as Marsala or Vin Santo, over the cake at the same time as you add the lemon juice.

¾ cup fine stoneground polenta flour

1 teaspoon baking powder

¼ teaspoon salt

1 cup unsalted butter, softened

1 cup plus 2 tablespoons superfine sugar

3 medium eggs

1 teaspoon vanilla extract

1 teaspoon almond extract

juice and finely shredded zest of 2 lemons

2¼ cups ground almonds

8-inch loose-bottom round cake pan, buttered, lined with parchment paper

Serves 6–8

This ice cream is based on one discovered by an epicurean colleague in a cafe in Trieste, in northeastern Italy. It is a superb, sumptuous ice cream, best served straight from the churn. Prepare it ahead, and leave chilled, but not frozen. Turn on your electric ice cream maker (churn type) between courses for perfect timing: it will be ready in 20 minutes. Serve with thin, bitter chocolates.

Gelato al caffè e caramello

Coffee and Toffee Ice Cream

Granita al melone
Melon granita

2 ripe cantaloupe melons, about
   1½ lb. each, peeled and seeded
6 tablespoons superfine sugar
juice of 1 orange
juice of 2–3 lemons
2 teaspoons orange flower water
Serves 4–6

Dice the melon flesh and mix in a blender or juicer (not a food processor —too lumpy). This should give about 3¾ cups liquid. Dissolve the sugar in the juice of the orange and 1 of the lemons, stirring until it dissolves. Add the orange flower water then stir into the fruit pulp. Taste. If too sweet, add more lemon juice. Freeze in ice-cube trays until solid, transfer to a food processor, and purée until frothy and pale. Refreeze in a covered container for 10 to 12 minutes before use.

4 tablespoons sugar, for the caramel
¾ cup strong, hot, freshly made coffee,
   such as arabica
1¾ cups heavy cream
1¾ cups light cream

2 vanilla beans, split lengthwise
4 medium egg yolks
¾ cup plus 2 tablespoons sugar

Serves 4–6

Caramelize the 4 tablespoons sugar in a dry skillet, over very high heat, shaking the skillet over the element but never stirring, until it reaches a mahogany color, then pour into a shallow metal tray to set. When set, break into pieces and dissolve them in the hot, freshly made coffee, then let cool.

    To make the custard, heat the two creams in a saucepan with the vanilla beans. Use a wooden spoon or stiff pastry brush to help prise out the tiny black vanilla seeds. When almost boiling, beat the egg yolks and the second measure of sugar until creamy and thick. Pour in the hot liquids, return the bowl contents to the pan and cook, stirring, over a gentle heat until the custard gently thickens. Do not let it boil.

    Chill over ice water, then freeze using an electric ice cream maker (churn type) for about 20 minutes or until set. Serve, if possible, immediately. Alternatively, pack into a covered container and refreeze. When ready to serve, soften in the refrigerator or at a cool room temperature for 15 to 20 minutes to produce a silky texture.

Note: In some parts of Italy ice cream is served in little sweet brioches instead of wafers, or with slices of warm panettone bread. Superb!

This is one of Italy's most famous desserts. Make it just before you want to serve it, and make sure you are well organized before you start—provide a green salad for your guests while you work in the kitchen or there may be a riot while they wait!

Zabaione

Warm Marsala Custard

5 egg yolks
1 whole egg
8 tablespoons superfine sugar
8 tablespoons Marsala wine

8–12 cantucci, savoiardi, amaretti, or *Brutti ma buoni* cookies (see right)

Serves 4–6

Combine the first 3 ingredients in a curved-bottom heatproof bowl or pitcher set over a pan of barely simmering water. Check the water level from time to time—it tends to evaporate. Do not overfill when you add more water—bowl and water must never touch.

Using an electric hand-held beater, balloon whisk, or rotary beater, beat the mixture until it becomes first a stable, light froth, and then of thick mousse-like consistency—about 10 to 15 minutes in all. Drizzle in spoonfuls of Marsala, continuing the same rhythm of beating all the time. Remove pan and bowl from the heat and continue beating until the froth will hold its shape and stay thick when the beaters are lifted out. Serve warm in tall goblets, elegant bowls, or pretty tumblers set on a small flat plate. Put several crisp cookies beside each for dipping into the warm dessert.

Variations:

1. Substitute half cream sherry and half dark rum instead of Marsala—superb!
2. Serve over a bed of seasonal berries.
3. To serve as a *Semifreddo de Zabaione*, whisk the warm zabaione until cool then fold gently into 1¼ cups of firmly whipped cream. Freeze (without stirring) in the freezer. To churn, do not whip the cream before folding together. Churn until set, about 20 minutes.

Brutti ma buoni Ugly-but-good cookies

1¼ lb. almond paste, coarsely grated
2 egg whites
2 oz. candied citron, cut up finely
2 oz. chopped candied orange peel
2 oz. chopped candied lemon peel
2 oz. unskinned almonds, chopped
2 oz. pignoli nuts
confectioners' sugar, for dusting
Makes 32

Beat the almond paste and egg whites together. Mix in the citron and peels. Chill 30 minutes. Take 1 teaspoon dough and roll it in one hand, pushing on some pignolis with the other. (Dust your hands with confectioners' sugar while rolling.) Place 2 inches apart on an ungreased baking tray. Bake in a preheated oven for 30 minutes at 300°F until golden and firm. Cool 5 minutes on the tray, then 15 minutes on wire racks. Store in an airtight jar. Serve, dusted with confectioners' sugar.

Index